I Follow Rules

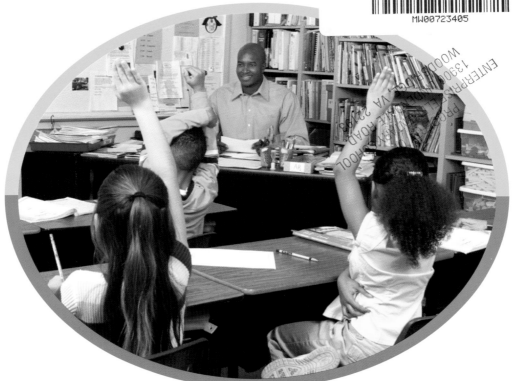

by Cynthia Swain

I need to know these words.

reading

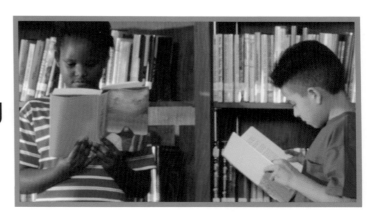

sitting

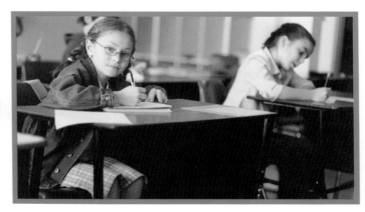

sweeping

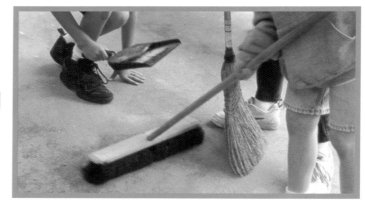

walking

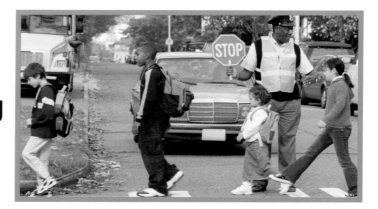

3

I am **walking**.

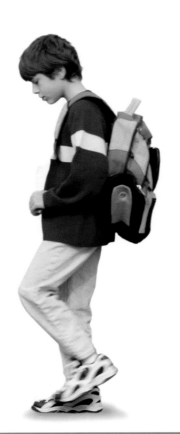

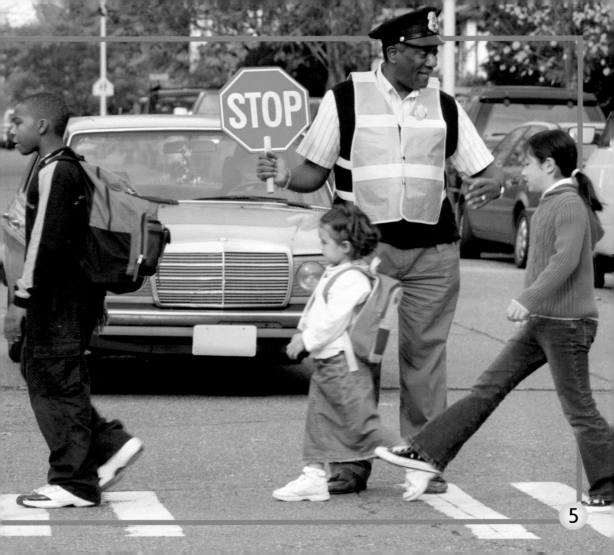

I am **sitting**.

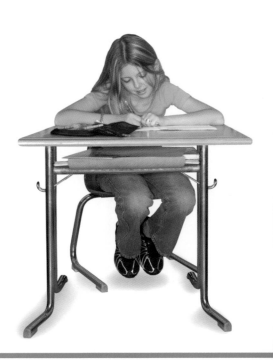

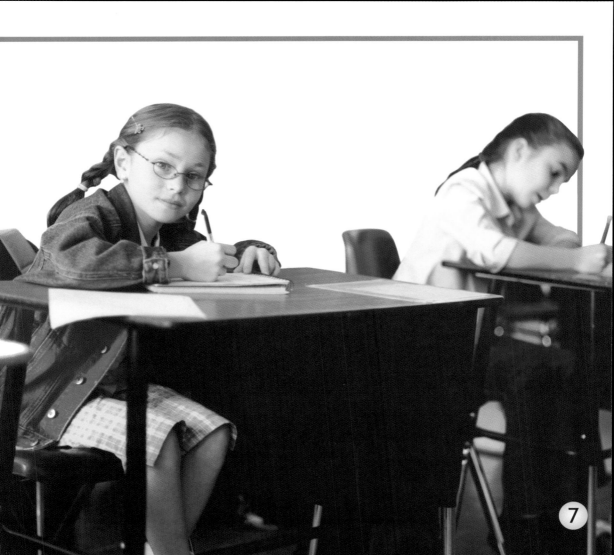

I am listening.

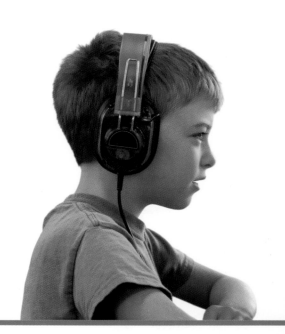

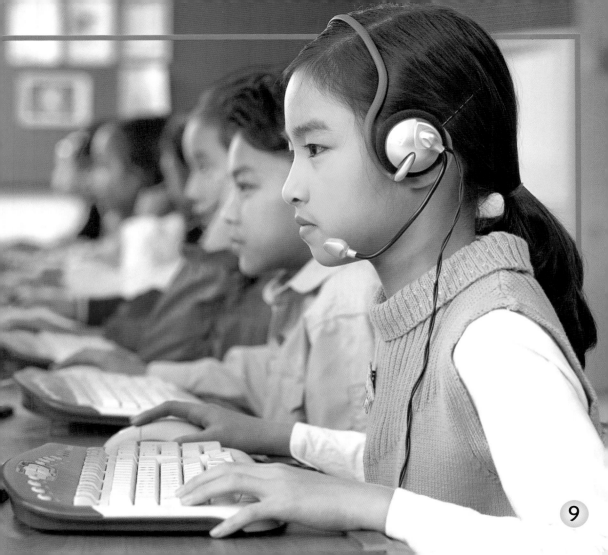

I am **reading**.

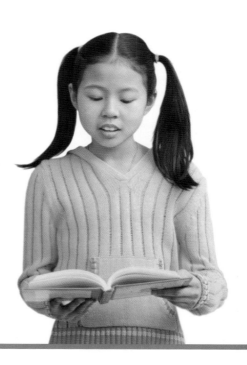

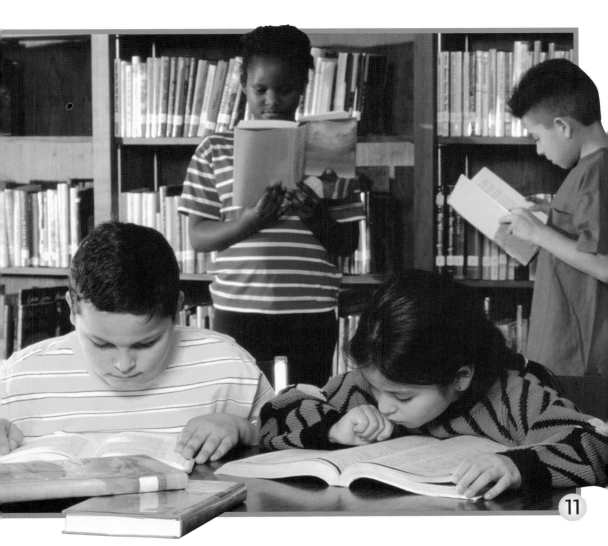

I am **sweeping**.

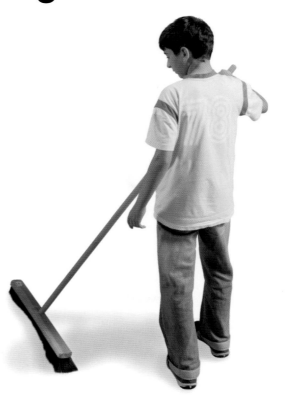

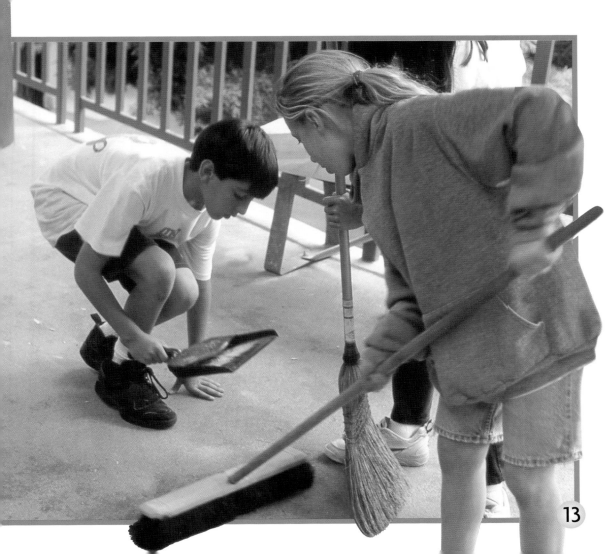

I am helping.

14

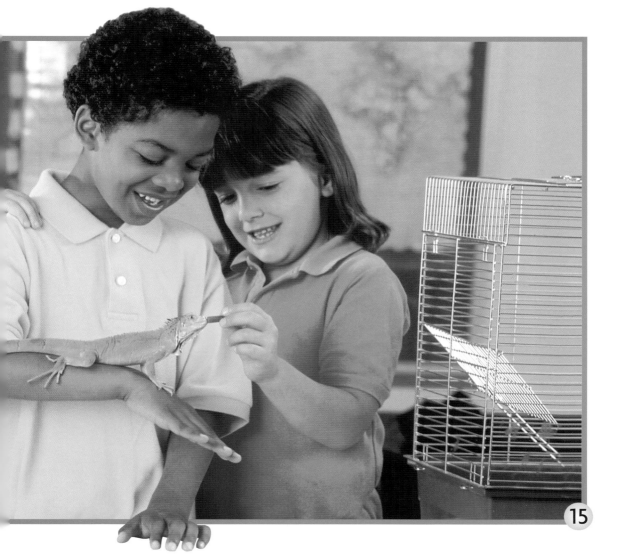

I am giving.

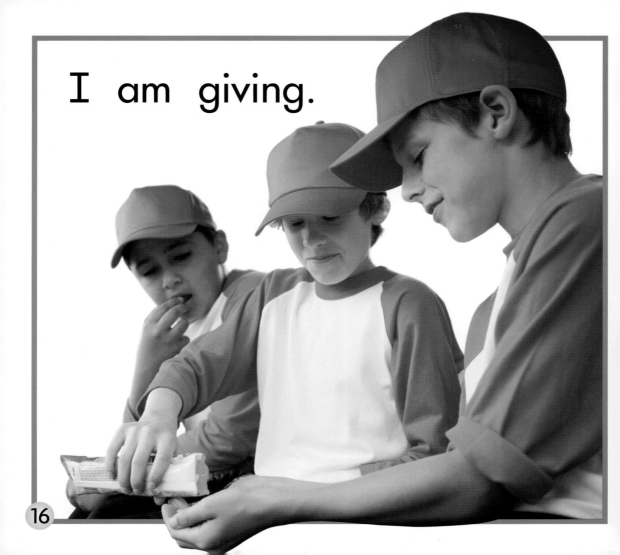